THE SARUM RITE

THE SARUM RITE
Sarum Breviary Noted

Sarum Compline: BCP English

Edited by William Renwick

GIC

THE GREGORIAN INSTITUTE OF CANADA
HAMILTON ONTARIO

ISBN 978-1-7752999-1-2

1 2 3 4 5 6 7 8 9 10   27 26 25 24 23 22 21 20 19 18

Introduction

THIS volume contains all of the texts and music required for the performance of the Sarum Office of Compline throughout the year. The principle sources are the *Breviarium* (1531), the *Antiphonale* (1519-20), and the facsimile *Antiphonale Sarisburiense* (1901-24). The translations follow the style of the *Book of Common Prayer* and the *King James Bible*. The full scholarly apparatus as well as a 'Companion' appear in the on-line edition at sarum-chant.ca. At the same location will be found the tones for the psalms and chapters.

The Feast of the Most Sweet Name of Jesus (Compline 23) was a late addition to the Sarum liturgical calendar dating to the latter half of the fifteenth century.

Compline is said standing, except for the preces, which are said kneeling on 'kneeling days' (see p. 63).

Preceding the office is said privately '*In the name of the our Lord* ✠ *Jesus Christ. Amen.*' or '*In the name of the Father* ✠ *and of the Son and of the Holy Ghost. Amen.*' The *Our Father* and *Hail Mary* that follow may be found on p. 55. The latter part of *Hail Mary*, which appears only in a small number of later Sarum sources, may be omitted.

The psalms and canticle are pointed to facilitate performance. The method of pointing employed here is fully described at sarum-chant.ca.

'Without note' indicated at Completorium 10 and 11, for psalm 51 in the ferial preces (p. 61), and 'For the Peace of the Church' (pp. 65-66), would appear to signify 'recto tono', that is, a monotone recitation.

Typically only the incipit of each antiphon is sung before the psalms and canticle; the full antiphon is sung at the end.

The rubrics do not always make perfectly clear whether Compline commences on the eve or on the day itself. Complines 1, 4, 7-9, 14, and

18-23 commence on the eve of the indicated day. Complines 2, 3, 5, 6, 10-13, and 15-17 commence on the day itself.

Compline 18 is said on both the eve and the day of all double feasts from octave of the Epiphany until the first Sunday of Lent and from Trinity to Advent unless a proper Compline be had (i.e. Complines 19-23). Compline 18 is likewise said on the eve of the Feast and throughout the octave of the Dedication.

If the feast of St. Gregory falls on Saturday before the first Sunday of Lent Compline 18 is said on the eve but Compline 7 is said on the day.

When the Full Service of the Blessed Virgin is sung the Christmas doxology 'All honour, laud, and glory be, O Jesu, Virgin-born' is used for the hymn. Likewise if the feast of the Annunciation falls within Eastertide the Christmas doxology is used for the hymn *Jesu, who brought'st redemption.* The Christmas doxology is also used for the feast and throughout the octave, when kept, of Corpus Christi.

Within the Octave of St. John the Baptist both the eve and the day of Sts. John and Paul (June 25 and 26) use Compline 6.

The feast of St. Anne uses Compline 18.

Within the octave of the Visitation, the feast of St. Martin, the octave of Sts. Peter and Paul, and the translation of St. Thomas the martyr use Compline 18.

On the eve of the Transfiguration Compline 18 is used, but with the Christmas doxology 'All honour, laud, and glory be, O Jesu, Virgin-born' for the hymn *Thee, Saviour of the world.*

The eve and the day of the Exaltation of the Holy Cross both use Compline 18.

Both the eve and the day of All Saints use Compline 19.

W.R.

Feast of St. Cuthbert, 2018.

❦ *At Compline.*

At Compline of the day throughout the whole year, having said Our Father. *and* Hail Mary. *privately, let the Priest begin.*

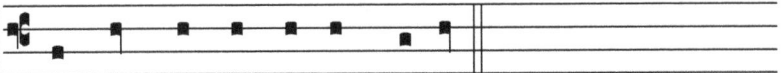

Urn us then, O God our Saviour.

Let the Choir respond thus.

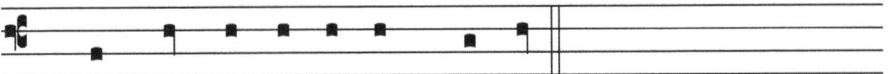

℟. And let thine anger cease from us.

1

The Officiant.

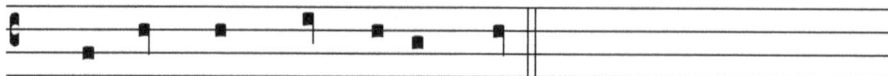

℣. O God, make speed to save me.

The Choir.

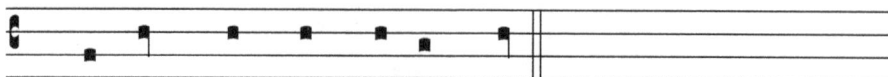

℟. O Lord, make haste to help me.

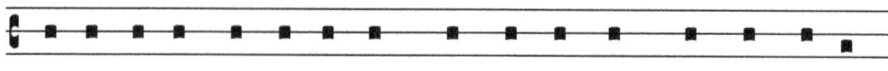

Glo-ry be to the Father, and to the Son, and to the Ho-ly

Ghost : as it was in the be-ginning, is now, and ev-er shall be :

world without end. Amen.   Alle-lu-ya.

And let it be concluded with Alleluya. *throughout the whole year except from First Vespers of Septuagesima Sunday until Easter : then indeed let this be sung in its place.*

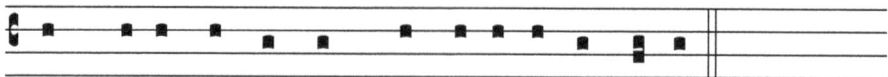

Praise be to thee, O Lord, King of e-ternal glo-ry.

Compline i.

❦ *During Advent.*

Miserere michi Domine.

Ant.
VIII.i.

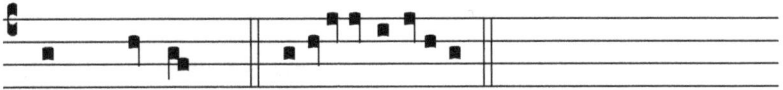

Ave mercy. *Ps.* Hear me when I call.

Psalm 4. Cum invocarem.

Ear me when I call, O God ōf my righteous-ness : thou hast set me at liberty when I was in trouble ; have mercy upon me, and hêarken untó my prayer.

2. O ye sons of men, how long will ye blasphême mine hónour : and have such pleasure in vanity, and sêek after léasing ?

3. Know this also, that the Lord hath chosen to himself the mân thāt is gódly : when I call upon the Lôrd, he will héar me.

4. Stand in âwe, and sín not : commune with your own heart, and in yōur châmber, ánd be still.

5. Offer the sacrifĉe of ríghteousness : and pūt your trúst in the Lord.

6. There be mâny thát say : Who wīll shêw us ány good ?

7. Lórd, líft thou up : the light of thy countēnânce upón us.

8. Thou hast put glâdness ín my heart : since the time that their corn, and wine, ānd ôil, incréased.

9. I will lay me down in pêace, and táke my rest : for it is thou, Lord, only, that makest mē dwêll in sáfety.

Glory be to the Fâthēr, and tó the Son : ānd tô the Hóly Ghost.

As it was in the beginning, is now, and êver sháll be : wôrld without énd. Amen.

3

Psalm 31. *In te Domine speravi. xxx.*

ℐN thee, O Lôrd, hãve I pút my trust : let me never be put to confusion, deliver mẽ ȋn thy ríghteousness.

2. Bow dȏwn thine eȃr to me : make hȃste to delíver me.

3. And be thou my strong rock, ãnd hoȗse óf defence : that thoȗ mȃyest sáve me.

4. For thou art my strong rock, ãnd my cástle : be thou also my guide, and lead mẽ fȏr thy Náme's sake.

5. Draw me out of the net that they have laid prȋvȋly fór me : for thoȗ árt my strength.

6. Into thy hands I commẽnd my spírit : for thou hast redeemed me, Õ Lôrd, thou Gód of truth.

Glory be to the Fȃthẽr, and tó the Son : ãnd tȏ the Hóly Ghost.

As it was in the beginning, is now, and ȇver sháll be : wȏrld without énd. Amen.

Psalm 91. *Qui habitat. xc.*

𝔚Hoso dwelleth under the defênce õf the móst High : shall abide under the shadow ȏf the Almíghty.

2. I will say unto the Lord, Thou art my hȏpe, ãnd my strónghold : my Gõd, in hȋm wíll I trust.

3. For he shall deliver thee from the snȃre õf the húnter : and from thẽ noȋsome péstilence.

4. He shall defend thee under his wings, and thou shalt be safe ûndẽr his féathers : his faith-

fulness and truth shall be thỹ shiêld and búckler.

5. Thou shalt not be afraid for any tẽrror bý night : nor for the arrow thãt flîeth bý day.

6. For the pestilence that wȃlkẽth in dárkness : nor for the sickness that destroyẽth ȋn the noón-day.

7. A thousand shall fall beside thee, and ten thousand ȃt thy right hand : but it shãll nȏt come nígh thee.

8. Yea, with thine êyes shalt

4

thóu behold : and see the reward ôf the ungódly.

9. For thôu, Lord, árt my hope : thou hast set thine house õf defênce véry high.

10. There shall no evil hãppen únto thee : neither shall any plague cõme nîgh thy dwélling.

11. For he shall give his angẽls chârge óver thee : to kêep thee in áll thy ways.

12. They shall bêar thee ín their hands : that thou hurt not thỹ fôot agáinst a stone.

13. Thou shalt go upon the lîõn and ádder : the young lion and the dragon shalt thou treãd ûnder thý feet.

14. Because he hath set his love upon me, therefore will Î̃ delíver him : I will set him up, becâuse he hath knówn my Name.

15. He shall call upon me, and Î̃ will heár him : yea, I am with him in trouble ; I will deliver him, and brĩng him to hónour.

16. With long life will I sãtisfý him : and shew hĭm mỹ salvátion.

Psalm 134. Ecce nunc. cxxxiij.

BEhôld now, praíse the Lord : all yẽ sêrvants óf the Lord ;

2. Ye that by night stand in thẽ hôuse óf the Lord : even in the courts of thẽ hôuse of óur God.

3. Lift up your hands in the sãnctuáry : ánd praíse the Lord.

4. The Lord that made hêaven

ánd earth : give thee blessĩng ôut of Síon.

Glory be to the Fâthẽr, and tó the Son : ãnd tô the Hóly Ghost.

As it was in the beginning, is now, and êver sháll be : wôrld without énd. Amen.

❡ *Let these aforesaid Psalms be sung daily at Compline throughout the whole year, whenever the service is made, except from Maundy Thursday until the Octave of Easter : and they are sung on one Tone with no Psalm elevated.*

Ant.

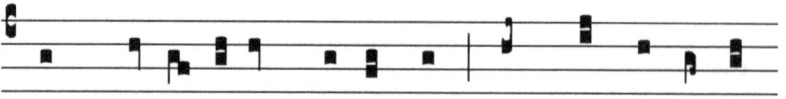

Ave mercy upon me, O Lord : and hearken unto

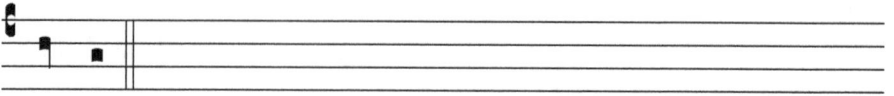

my prayer.

❦ *The preceding Antiphon is sung on these Psalms throughout the whole of Advent, and from the morrow of the Octave of the Epiphany until Lent, and from Passion Sunday until Maundy Thursday, and from the morrow of Trinity Sunday until Advent, except on the Feasts and during the Octaves of the Name of Jesus and of Blessed Mary, and not on the Feast of Relics nor on the Feast of All Saints.*

Chapter. Jeremiah xiv. 9.

THou, O Lord, art in the midst of us, and we are called by thy holy Name : leave us not, O Lord our God. ℟. Thanks be to God.

This Chapter is said at Compline throughout the whole year except from Maundy Thursday until the Octave of Easter.

Let this Hymn be sung to the following Melody on all Sundays and on Simple Feasts with Rulers of the Choir and on Commemorations of Blessed Mary and on the Feast of the Place and on any Octave days and during any Octaves with Rulers of the Choir when this Hymn is appointed to be sung at Compline, except when the Hymn is of the feria.

Te lucis ante terminum.

Hymn.
VIII.

O thee, be-fore the close of day, * Cre-a-tor of the

world we pray : That with thy won-ted fa-vour thou Wouldst

be our guard and keeper now. 2. From all ill dreams de-fend

our eyes, From nightly fears and fantasies : Tread under

foot our ghostly foe, That no pollution we may know.

3. O Father, that we ask be done, Through Je-sus Christ

thine only Son : Who, with the Ho- ly Ghost and thee,

Doth live and reign e-ternal-ly.   Amen.

On Commemorations of Blessed Mary when this Hymn is sung let this

Verse be sung.

3. All honour, laud, and glo-ry be,　O Je-su, Vir-gin-born, to

thee : All glo-ry, as　is ev-er meet, To Father and to

Pa-raclete.　Amen.

This following Melody is sung on all ferias and on Feasts of Three Lessons without Rulers of the Choir when a Hymn is sung at Compline.

Hymn.
VIII.

O thee, be-fore the close of day, * Cre-a-tor of the

world, we pray, That with thy wonted fa-vour, thou Wouldst

be our guard and keeper now. 2. From all ill dreams de-fend

our eyes, From nightly fears and fantasies : Tread under

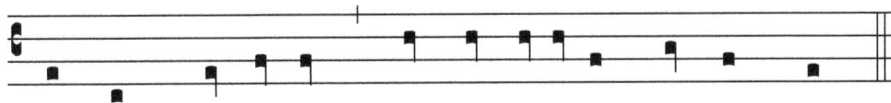

foot our ghostly foe, That no pollution we may know.

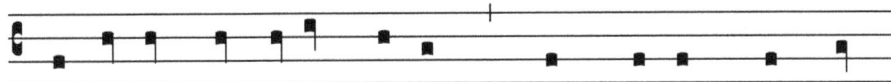

3. O Father, that we ask be done, Through Je-sus Christ thine

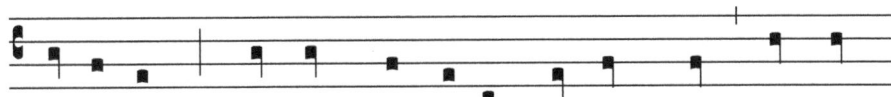

only Son : Who, with the Ho-ly Ghost and thee, Doth live

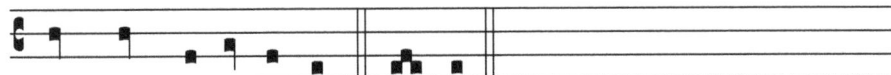

and reign e-ternal-ly.   A-men.

Custodi nos Domine.

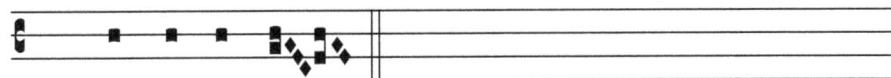

℣. Keep us, O Lord.

℟. *privately.* As the apple of an eye, hide us under the shadow of thy wings.

❦ *At Compline during the whole of Advent let the following Antiphon be sung on the Psalm* Nunc dimittis.

Veni Domine.

Ant.
VII.i.

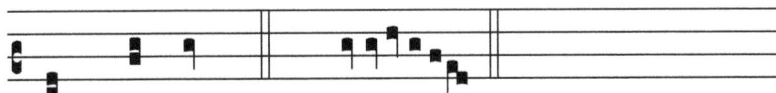

Ome, O Lord.   *Ps.* Lord, now lettest.

The Song of Simeon. Luke ij. 29. Nunc dimittis.

Ord, now lettest thou thy sêrvãnt depárt in peace : ãccôrding tó thy word.

2. Fôr mine éyes have seen : thŷ sálvátion.

3. Which thou hãst prepáred : before the fãce of all péople.

4. To be a light to lîghtẽn the Géntiles : and to be the glory of thŷ péople Ísrael.

Glory be to the Fãthẽr, and tó the Son : ãnd tô the Hóly Ghost.

As it was in the beginning, is now, and êver sháll be : wôrld without énd. Amen.

Ant.

Ome, O Lord, and vi-sit us in peace : that we may joy be-fore thee with a perfect heart.

Kyrie eleyson. &c. *Here follow the Preces.* 55.

❧ *This Compline is not altered in Advent except on Double Feasts that fall within Advent : then indeed only the Hymn is changed, and the Hymn* Thee, Saviour of the world. ii. *is sung : and except on Commemorations of Blessed Mary that are celebrated in Advent : then indeed at the end of the Hymn is sung* All honour . . . O Jesu, Virgin-born, to thee. 8.

Compline 2.

❧ *On the Vigil of the Nativity of the Lord at Compline on the Psalms. Let one of the Superior Grade at his place begin the Antiphon.*

Estote parati.

Ant. VIII.i.

B E ye ready, * like unto men that wait for the Lord, when he will re-turn from the wedding.

Ps. Hear me when I call. *and the Psalms that follow.* 3.

Chapter. Thou, O Lord. 6.

❧ *If it be asked whether at any time in the Choir of Sarum another Melody is sung on the Hymn* Thee, Saviour of the world. *of which the following is the Melody, the answer is no, except on three days in the Week of the Nativity, that is to say Saint Stephen, Saint John, and the Holy Innocents, which are outside the rule : on which days any Melody for no matter which Hymn may be introduced for those three Solemnities as celebrated and permitted from ancient times : that is to say at the discretion of the Deacons, the Priests, and the boys.*

Salvator mundi Domine.

Hymn. VII.

T Hee, Saviour of the world, we pray, * Who hast pre-

11

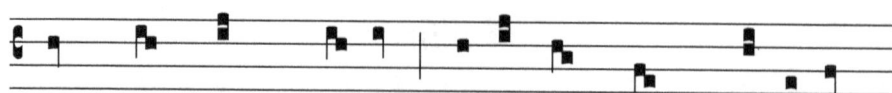

served us through the day, Pro-tect us through the coming

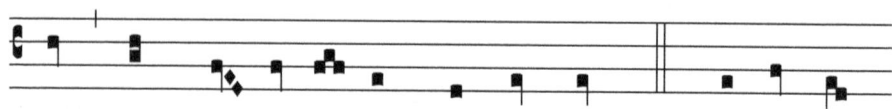

night, And save us al-way, Lord of might. 2. Be with us

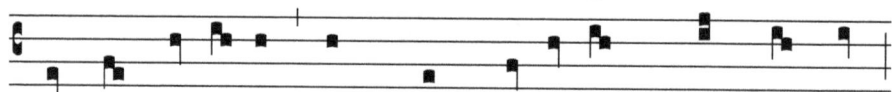

now, in mercy nigh, And spare thy servants when they cry,

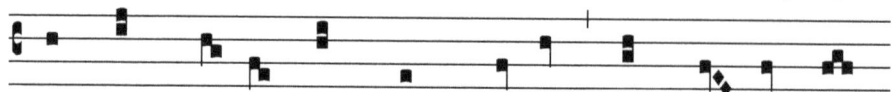

Our sins blot out, our prayers re-ceive, Our darkness light-

en, and forgive. 3. O let not sleep o'ercome the soul, Nor

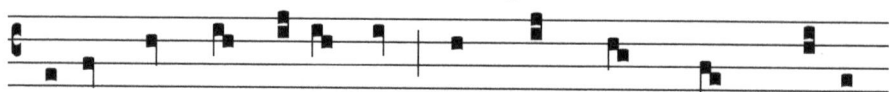

Sa-tan with his spi-rits foul : Our flesh keep chaste, that it

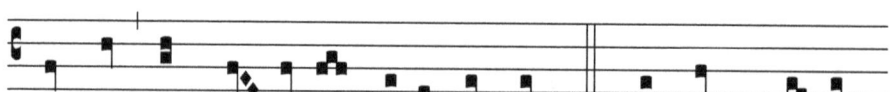

may be, An ho- ly temple unto thee. 4. To thee, who dost

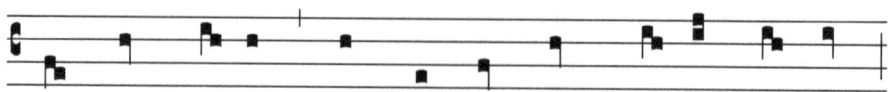

our souls re-new, With heartfelt vows we humbly sue,

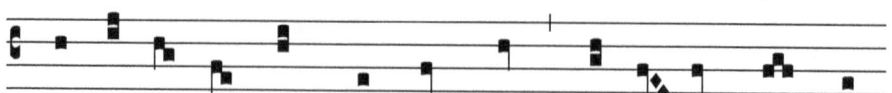

That pure in heart, and free from stain, We from our beds may rise a-gain. 5. All laud to God the Father be ; All praise, E-

ternal Son, to thee ; All glo-ry, as is e-ver meet, To God

the Ho- ly Pa-raclete. A-men.

❡ *On the day of the Nativity of the Lord at Compline after Second Vespers and from thence until the Feast of the Epiphany after both Vespers and also on the Feasts of the Assumption, the Nativity, the Purification, and the Conception of Blessed Mary, and during their Octaves, is sung the ℣.*

5. All honour, laud, and glo-ry be,   O Je-su, Virgin-born, to

thee; All glo-ry, as is e-ver meet, To Fa-ther and to

Pa-raclete. A-men.

On the Feast of the Epiphany and during its Octave is sung the ℣.

5. All honour, Lord, to thee we pay For thine E-pipha-ny

(musical notation)

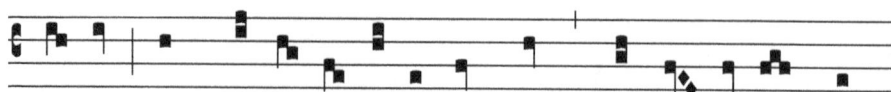

to-day : All glo-ry, as is e-ver meet, To Fa-ther and to

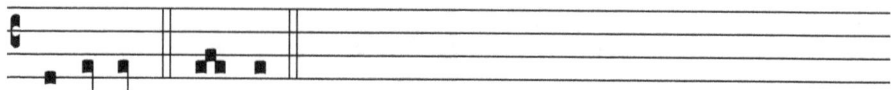

(musical notation)

Pa-raclete. A-men.

On the Vigil of Pentecost and during the week itself are sung the ℣℣.

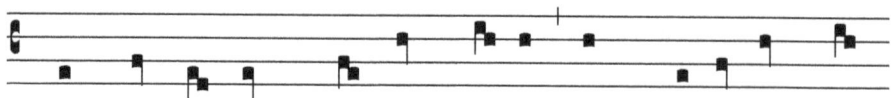

(musical notation)

5. As then, O Lord, thou didst ful-fil, Each ho-ly heart to

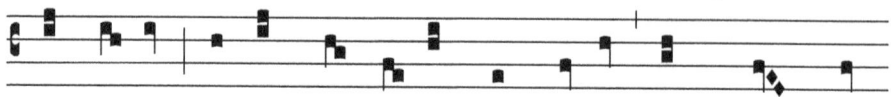

(musical notation)

do thy will, So now do thou our sins forgive And make the

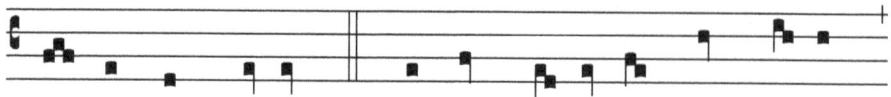

(musical notation)

world in peace to live. 6. To God the Father, God the Son,

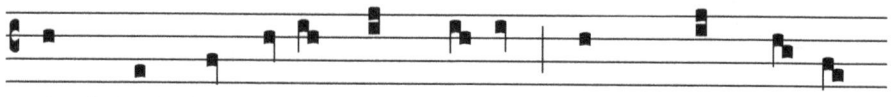

(musical notation)

And God the Spi-rit, praise be done : And Christ the Lord

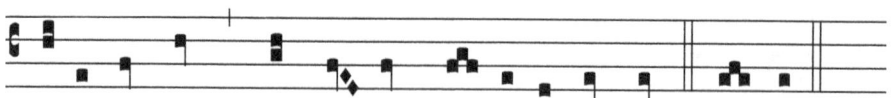

(musical notation)

upon us pour The Spi- rit's gift for ev-ermore. A-men.

❡ *This Hymn is sung at Compline of the day until the Octave Day of the Epiphany and during that Octave and on all Double Feasts from the Octave of the Epiphany until the First Sunday of Lent, and on all Double Feasts from the Vigil of Pentecost until the Vigil of the Nativity of the Lord, except on the Feast and during the Octave of the Name of Jesus when the service is of the Octave, but it is nevertheless sung on Feasts of Nine Lessons that occur within that Octave. It is likewise sung on the Vigil of Pentecost and on the Thursday, Friday, and Saturday of the week of Pentecost, and daily during the Octaves and on the Octave Days of the Assumption and of the Nativity of Blessed Mary and of the Dedication of the Church, unless the Feast of the Dedication of the Church falls within Lent or Passiontide, if the service is of the Octave or of any Saint of Nine Lessons, and during the Octave of Corpus Christi when it is observed with Rulers of the Choir.*

Let one boy from the Choir side, changing neither place nor vestment, sing the ℣. Keep us, O Lord. 9.

Let one of the more senior persons from the Choir Side at the discretion of the Ruler begin the Antiphon.

Vigilate omnes.

Ant.
IV.i.

Atch, all ye, * and pray, for ye know not

when the time is. Watch ye there-fore, for ye know not

when the mas-ter of the house com- eth, at e-ven, or at

midnight, or at the cockcrowing, or in the mor-ning : lest

15

coming suddenly, he   find you sleep-   ing.

Ps. Lord, now lettest. 10.

Let the Preces &c. that pertain to Compline conclude the service. 55.

Compline 3.

❦ *On the day of the Nativity of the Lord at Compline on the Psalms.*
Natus est nobis.

Ant.
VIII.i

N-to us is born * this day a Sa-viour, which is

Christ the Lord : in the ci-ty of Da-vid. *Ps.* Hear me when I
call. *and the Psalms that follow.* 3.

Chapter. Thou, O Lord. 6.

Hymn. Thee, Saviour of the World. 11.

℣. Keep us, O Lord. 9.

Alleluya. Verbum caro.

Ant.
V.i.

L-le-lu- ya. * The Word was made flesh, al-le-lu-ya : and dwelt among us, al-le-lu- ya, al-le- lu- ya.

Ps. Lord, now lettest. 10.

Let the Preces &c. that pertain to Compline conclude the service. 55.

This Compline is not changed until the Circumcision. However the Antiphon on Nunc Dimittis. *is sung until the Vigil of the Epiphany.*

Compline 4.

❦ *On the eve of the Circumcision of the Lord at Compline.*

Nato Domino.

Ant.
VIII.i.

T the Lord's * na-ti-vi-ty, the choirs of angels chan-

ted say-ing : Salvation to our God, seated on the

throne, and to the Lamb. *Ps.* Hear me when I call. *and the Psalms that follow.* 3.

Chapter. Thou, O Lord. 6.

Hymn. Thee, Saviour of the World. 11.

℣. Keep us, O Lord. 9.

Ant. Alleluya. The Word was made flesh. 16. *Ps.* Nunc dimittis. 10.

Let the Preces &c. that pertain to Compline conclude the service. 55.

This Compline is not changed until the Vigil of the Epiphany.

Compline 5.

❦ *On the Vigil of the Epiphany at Compline on the Psalms.*
Lux de luce.

Ant.
VIII.ii.

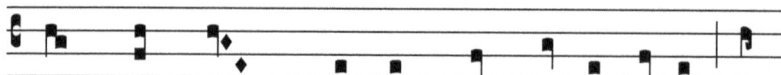

Ight from Light, * thou, O Christ, hast appeared : un-

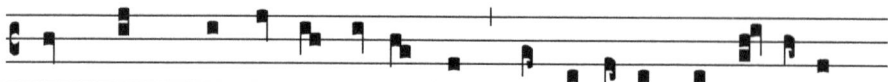

to whom the Sa-ges offer gifts, al-le-lu-ya, al-le- lu-ya,

al-le-lu-ya. *Ps.* Hear me when I call. *and the Psalms that follow.*
3.

Chapter. Thou, O Lord. 6.
Hymn. Thee, Saviour of the World. 11.
℣. Keep us, O Lord. 9.

Alleluya. Omnes de Saba.

Ant.
V.i.

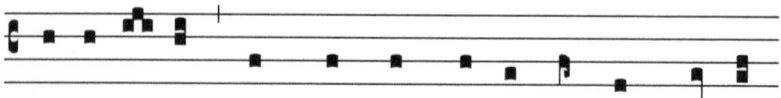

L-le-lu- ya. * All they from Sa-ba shall come, al-le-

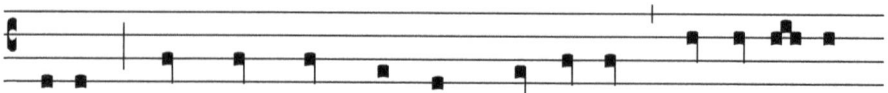

lu-ya : they shall bring gold and frankincense, al-le-lu- ya,

18

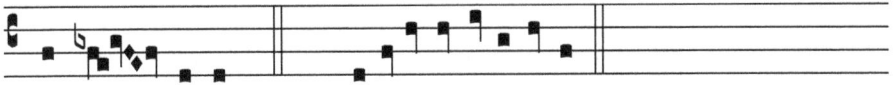

al-le- lu-ya. *Ps.* Lord, now lettest. 10.

Let the Preces &c. that pertain to Compline conclude the service. 55.

This Compline is not changed during the whole Octave.

Compline 6.

℟ *On the morrow of the Octave of the Epiphany at Compline.*

Ant. Have mercy upon me. 3.

Ps. Hear me when I call. *and the Psalms that follow.* 3.

Chapter. Thou, O Lord. 6.

Hymn. To thee, before the close of day. 7-8.

℣. Keep us, O Lord. 9.

Salva nos.

Ant.
III.iv.

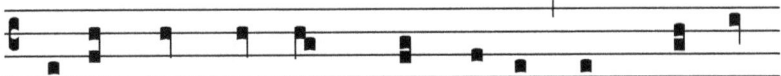

Re-serve us, * O Lord, while wa-king, and guard us

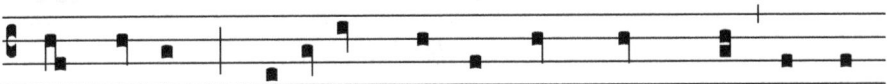

while sleeping : that awake we may watch with Christ, and a-

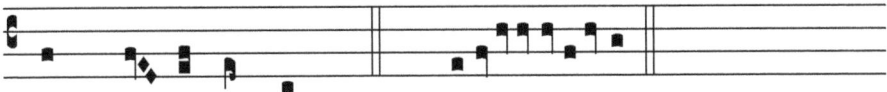

sleep may rest in peace. *Ps.* Lord, now lettest. 10.

Let the Preces &c. that pertain to Compline conclude the service. 55.

This Compline is said from the morrow of the Octave of the Epiphany

19

until the First Sunday in Lent and from the morrow of the Holy Trinity until the Advent of the Lord except on Double Feasts and during the Octaves of the Visitation, Assumption, and Nativity of Blessed Mary, and the Dedication of the Church, and the Name of Jesus, and Corpus Christi, where the Octaves are observed with Rulers of the Choir, and except on Commemorations of St. Mary, and during Octaves of the Feast of the Place where Vespers is observed with Rulers of the Choir.

Compline 7.

❡ *The First Sunday of Lent at Compline on the Psalms.*

Signatum est.

Ant.
VI.

Ift thou up * O Lord, the light of thy counten-ance

upon us : thou, O Lord, hast put gladness in my heart.

Ps. Hear me when I call. *and the Psalms that follow.* 3.

Chapter. Thou, O Lord. 6.

In pace in idipsum.

The Clerk.

Resp.
VIII.

N per-fect

20

Let the Choir continue.

* peace and safe-ty. †I shall sleep, and take my rest.

The Clerk.

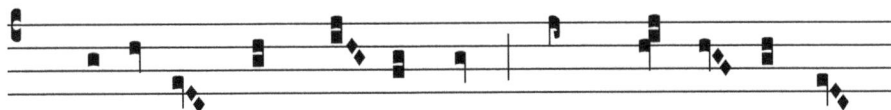

℣. If I give sleep to mine eyes : and slumber to mine

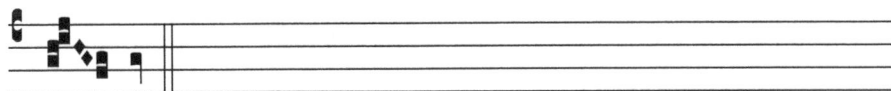

eye- lids.

The Choir.

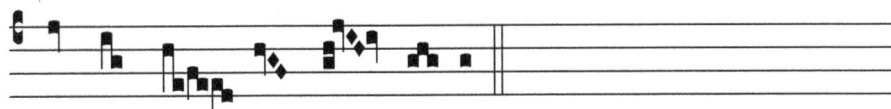

†I shall sleep, and take my rest.

The Clerk.

℣. Glo-ry be to the Father and to the Son : and to the

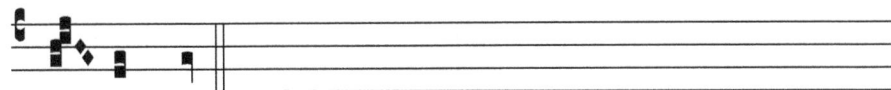

Ho- ly Ghost.

The Choir.

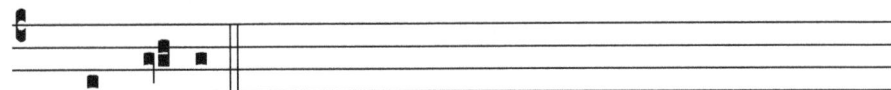

℟. In per-fect.

Christe qui lux est et dies.

Hymn.
II.

Christ, who art the Light and Day, * Thou driv-

est darksome night away ! We know thee as the Light of

light, Il-lumi-na-ting mortal sight. 2. All ho-ly Lord,

we pray to thee, Keep us to-night from danger free ; Grant

us, dear Lord, in thee to rest, So be our sleep in qui- et

blest. 3. Let not dull sleep the soul oppress, Nor crafty foe

the heart possess : Nor Sa-tan's wiles the flesh al-lure, To

make us in thy sight impure. 4. And while our eyes soft

slumber take, Still be the heart to thee awake ; By thy

right hand upheld a-bove Thy servants resting in thy

love. 5. Yea, our De-fender, be thou nigh To bid the

pow'rs of darkness fly ; Keep us from sin, and guide for

good Thy servants purchased by thy Blood. 6. Remember

us, dear Lord, we pray, While in this mortal flesh we

stay : 'Tis thou who dost the soul de-fend — Be pre-sent with

us to the end. 7. All laud to God the Father be ; All praise,

e-ternal Son, to thee : All glo-ry, as is e-ver meet, To God

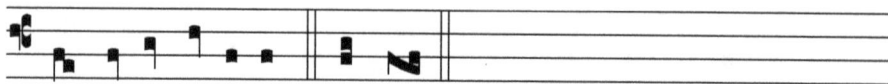

the Ho-ly Pa-raclete. Amen.

℣. Keep us, O Lord. 9.

Cum videris.

Ant.
IV.ii.

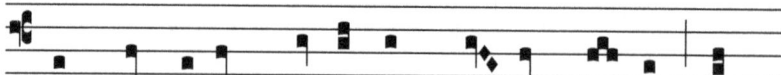

Hen thou se-est the na-ked, *co- ver thou him : and

hide not thy-self from thine own flesh : then shall thy light

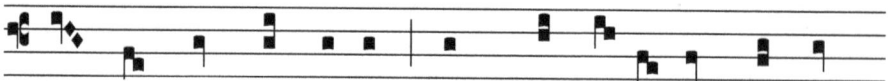

break forth as the morning : and the glo-ry   of the Lord

shall be thy re-ward. *Ps.* Lord, now lettest. 10.

Let the Preces &c. that pertain to Compline conclude the service. 55.

Let the preceding Antiphon, that is Lift thou up. *and the* ℟. In perfect peace. *and the Hymn* O Christ, who art. *be sung daily at Compline until the Passion of the Lord whatever service is made, but the Antiphon on the Psalm* Nunc dimittis. *for only fifteen days.*

❡ *It is understood that whenever any Feast shall be celebrated in Quadragesima nothing of the Lenten Compline shall be altered.*

Compline 8.

❦ *The Third Sunday of Lent at Compline, Antiphon.* Lift thou up. 20.

Ps. Hear me when I call. *and the Psalms that follow.* 3.

Chapter. Thou, O Lord. 6.

℟. In perfect peace. 20.

Hymn. O Christ, who art. 22.

℣. Keep us, O Lord. 9.

Media vite.

Ant.
IV.iii.

I N the midst of life * we are in death : of whom may

we seek for succour, but of thee, O Lord, who for our of-

fen-ces art justly dis-pleas-ed. †O ho- ly God.

‡O Ho- ly and mighty. ††O Ho- ly and merci-

ful Sa-viour : de-li-ver us not unto bit- ter death.

Ps. Lord, now lettest. 10. ℣. Cast us not a-way in the time of old age : when our strength fail-eth us, forsake us not, O Lord. †O Ho- ly God. ℣. Shut not thine ears to our pe-ti- tions. ‡O Ho- ly and mighty. ℣. Thou that knowest the se-crets of the heart : spare us from our sins. ††O Ho- ly and merci-ful.

Let the Preces &c. that pertain to Compline conclude the service. 55.

The preceding Antiphon is sung on the Psalm Nunc dimíttis. *for fifteen days. The Verses however are not sung, except on Saturdays and Sundays and on Feasts of Nine Lessons : and then the first and third Verses are sung*

26

by a single Clerk from the Choir Side, but the second Verse is sung by a single Clerk from the other side of the Choir, in such a way that on Saturday they are sung by the Superior Grade, and on Sunday by the Second Form : similarly on Feasts with Nine Lessons. However on Double Feasts at either Compline they are sung by the Superior Grade, changing neither place nor vestment.

When the ℣℣. of the preceding Antiphon In the midst of life. *or the following Antiphon* O King, all glorious. *are sung, the Antiphon will always be begun again after the Psalm-Verse has been sought from the Cantor. On Simple Feasts let two Rulers of the Choir together inquire, but on Principal Feasts the two Principal Rulers.*

Compline 9.

❡ *On Passion Sunday at Compline.*

   Ant. Have mercy upon me. 3.

   Ps. Hear me when I call. *and the Psalms that follow.* 3.

   Chapter. Thou, O Lord. 6.

In manus tuis.

Clerk.

Resp.
VI.

N-to thy hands,

Let the Choir continue.

O Lord, †I commend my spi-rit.

The Clerk.

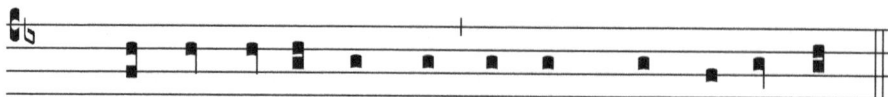

℣. Thou hast re-deemed me,   O Lord, thou God of truth.

The Choir.

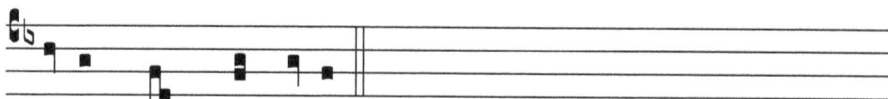

†I commend my spi-rit.

The ℣. Gloria Patri. *is not sung, but let the Cantor begin again* Into thy hands.

Cultor Dei memento.

Hymn.
VIII.

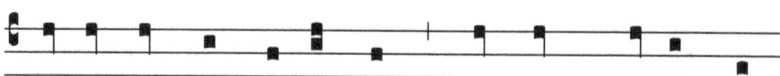

Ervant of God, remember * The stream thy soul be-

dew-ing, The grace that came upon thee   Anointing and

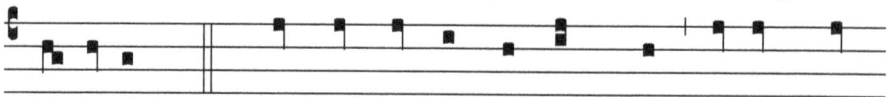

re-newing. 2. When kindly slumber calls thee, Upon thy

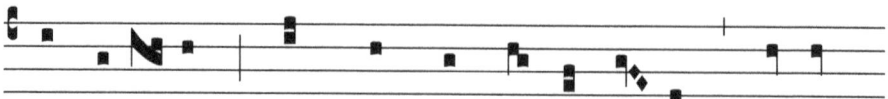

bed reclin- ing, Trace thou the Cross of Je- sus, Thy heart

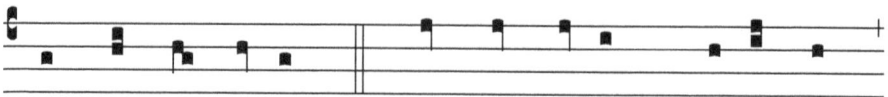

and forehead signing. 3. The Cross dissolves the darkness,

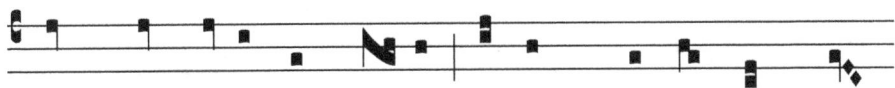

And drives away tempta-tion ; It calms the waver-ing spi-

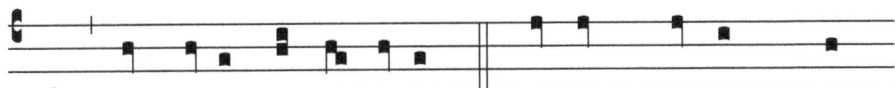

rit By qui- et conse-cration. 4. Be-gone, be-gone, the

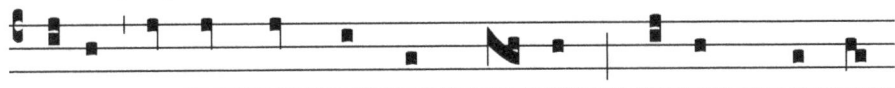

terrors Of vague and formless dream-ing ; Be-gone, thou fell

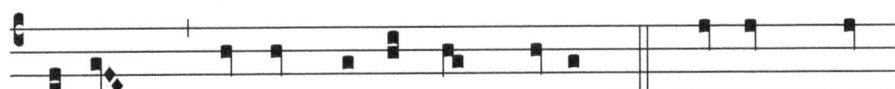

de-ceiv-er, With all thy boasted scheming. 5. Be-gone, thou

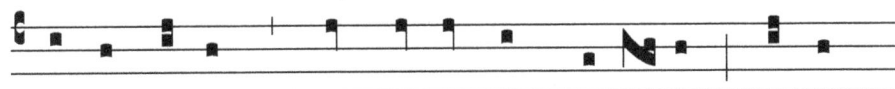

crooked serpent, Who, twist-ing and pursu- ing, By fraud

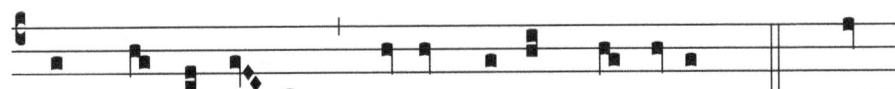

and lie pre-par- est The simple soul's undo- ing ; 6. Trem-

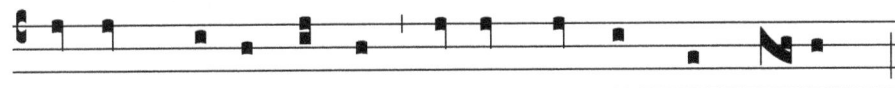

ble, for Christ is near us, De-part, for here he dwel-leth,

And this, the Sign thou know-est, Thy strong battal-

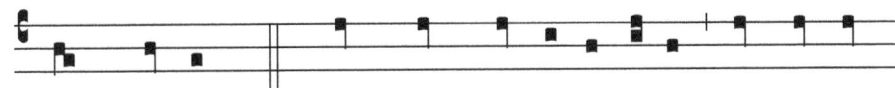

ions quel-leth. 7. Then while the weary body   Its rest in sleep is near-ing, The heart will muse in si- lence On

Christ and his appearing. 8. To God, e-ternal Father, To

Christ, our King, be glo- ry, And to the Ho-ly Spi- rit,

In ne-ver-ending sto-ry. Amen.

℣. Keep us, O Lord. 9.

O Rex gloriose.

Ant.
III.iv.

King, * all glo-ri- ous a-mid thy saintly compa-ny,

who ev-er shalt be praised, yet exceedest all ut-ter-ance :

thou, O Lord, art in the midst of us, and we are cal- led

by thy ho-ly Name ; leave us not, O our God : that in the

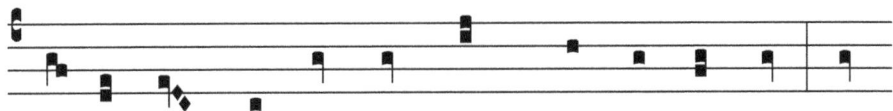

day of judgement it may please thee to place us. †A-

mong thy saints and cho-sen ones. ‡O blessed King.

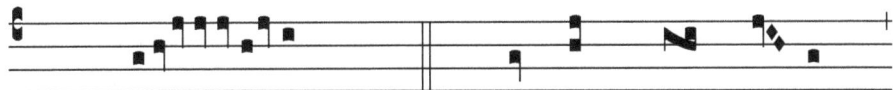

Ps. Lord, now lettest. 10. ℣. O King most bles-sed,

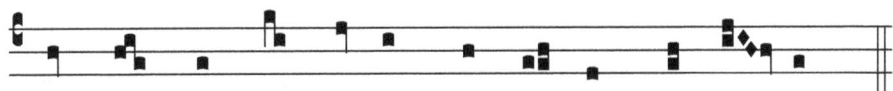

we pray thee to prosper the way of thy ser- vants.

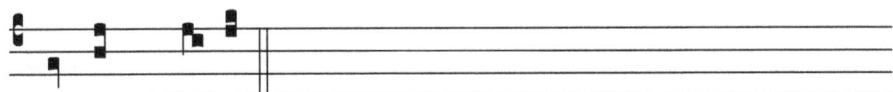

†Among thy saints.

Another Verse.

℣. That by God- ly discipline we may ef-face our grie-vous

offen- ces. ‡O blessed King. ℣. And so with pure con-

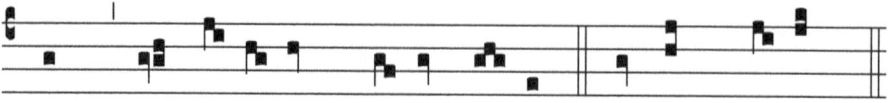

science may du- ly keep the Paschal feast. †Among thy saints.

to the end of the Antiphon.

Let the Preces &c. that pertain to Compline conclude the service. 55.

This Compline is not changed, but is said daily until first Vespers of Maundy Thursday, as indicated above, whatever the service, except that on ferias the Verses are not sung after the Psalm Nunc dimittis. *: in such a way that on Saturday the Verses are sung by the Superior Grade, and on Sunday by the Second Form. On Palm Sunday at both Complines they are sung by the Superior Grade. Similarly, on Double Feasts that occur within Passiontide and on the Wednesday before Easter they are sung by the Second Form.*

Compline 10.

❡ *On Maundy Thursday at Compline first let the beginning of the Antiphon* Christ became obedient. *be commenced by the Officiant without note. Then follow the Psalms* Hear me when I call. In thee, O Lord. Behold now. 3. *and Psalm* Nunc dimittis. 10. *without* Gloria Patri. *After the Psalms is said the whole Antiphon* Christ became obedient for us unto death, even the death of the cross.

Then let the Priest say ℣. The Lord be with you. ℟. And with thy spirit.

℣. Let us pray.

Prayer.

Look down, we beseech thee, O Lord, upon this thy family : for which our Lord Jesus Christ hesitated not to be delivered up into the hands of wicked men : and to undergo the torment of the cross. Who liveth and reigneth with thee in the unity of the Holy Ghost, one God, world without end. ℟.

32

Amen.

℣. The Lord be with you. ℞. And with thy spirit.
℣. Let us bless the Lord. ℞. Thanks be to God.

Compline ɪɪ.

❡ *On Good Friday at Compline let the Priest begin the Antiphon* Christ became obedient. 32. *without note. Meanwhile let the Choir kneel. The Antiphon and all the rest are said as on Maundy Thursday, without* The Lord be with you. *and without* Let us pray. *Following the Psalms and the Antiphon is said* Our Father. *and* Hail Mary. 55. *and the Psalm* Have mercy upon me. *without* Gloria Patri. *while kneeling.*

Psalm 51. Miserere mei Deus. l.

Have mercy upon me, O God, after thy great goodness : according to the multitude of thy mercies do away mine offences.

2. Wash me throughly from my wickedness : and cleanse me from my sin.

3. For I acknowledge my faults : and my sin is ever before me.

4. Against thee only have I sinned, and done this evil in thy sight : that thou mightest be justified in thy saying, and clear when thou art judged.

5. Behold, I was shapen in wickedness : and in sin hath my mother conceived me.

6. But lo, thou requirest truth in the inward parts : and shalt make me to understand wisdom secretly.

7. Thou shalt purge me with hyssop, and I shall be clean : thou shalt wash me, and I shall be whiter than snow.

8. Thou shalt make me hear of joy and gladness : that the bones which thou hast broken may rejoice.

9. Turn thy face from my sins : and put out all my misdeeds.

10. Make me a clean heart, O God : and renew a right spirit within me.

33

11. Cast me not away from thy presence : and take not thy holy Spirit from me.

12. O give me the comfort of thy help again : and stablish me with thy free Spirit.

13. Then shall I teach thy ways unto the wicked : and sinners shall be converted unto thee.

14. Deliver me from blood-guiltiness, O God, thou that art the God of my health : and my tongue shall sing of thy right-eousness.

15. Thou shalt open my lips, O Lord : and my mouth shall shew thy praise.

16. For thou desirest no sacri-fice, else would I give it thee : but thou delightest not in burnt-offerings.

17. The sacrifice of God is a troubled spirit : a broken and contrite heart, O God, shalt thou not despise.

18. O be favourable and gracious unto Sion : build thou the walls of Jerusalem.

19. Then shalt thou be pleased with the sacrifice of righteousness, with the burnt-offerings and ob-lations : then shall they offer young bullocks upon thine altar.

And let Compline be concluded with the Priest saying the Prayer Look down, we beseech thee. 32. *without* The Lord be with you. *and without* Let us pray. *without* Who liveth. *and without* Let us bless the Lord. *and thus let it be concluded.*

Compline 12.

❡ *On Holy Saturday on the Vigil of Easter at the signal of ringing the Bells with two strokes twice or thrice let the Priest begin* O God, make speed to save me. 2. Gloria Patri. *&c. in the usual manner, without* Turn us, O God.

Let the Antiphon be begun by one of the Superior Grade.

Alleluya. iiij.

Ant.
VII.vi.

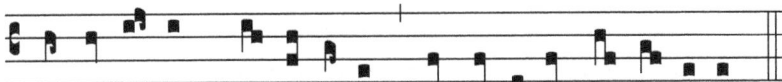

A-L-le-lu- ya, * al-le-lu-ya, al-le-lu-ya, al-le-lu-ya.

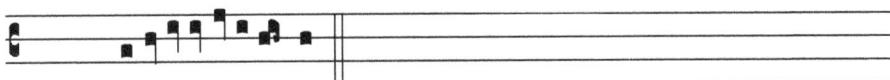

Ps. Hear me when I call. In thee, O Lord. Behold now. 3. Nunc dimittis. 10.

And these foregoing Psalms are sung under a single Tone with no Psalm elevated, which likewise is to be observed daily until the Octave of Easter at Compline. After ending the Psalms with Gloria Patri. *the whole Antiphon is sung.*

Then is said The Lord be with you. *and* Let us pray.

Prayer.

Pour forth upon us, O Lord, the spirit of thy love, that whom thou hast satisfied with the Paschal sacrament, thou mayest make by thy goodness to be of one mind. Through Jesus Christ thy Son our Lord, who liveth and reigneth in the unity of the same Holy Ghost, one God, world without end. ℟. Amen.

with The Lord be with you. *and* Let us bless the Lord. 63. *without* Alleluya. *by the Officiant.*

And it is understood that this Prayer Pour forth upon us. *is said daily at Compline until the Octave of Easter.*

Compline 13.

❡ *On Easter Day at Compline* O God, make speed to save me. 2. *Antiphon and Psalms as on Holy Saturday.* 35.

The Antiphon having been completed after the Psalms, immediately let be begun by the Cantor and continued by the Choir, without Neuma.

Hec dies.

Grad.
II.

His * is the day which the Lord hath

made : we will re-joice and be

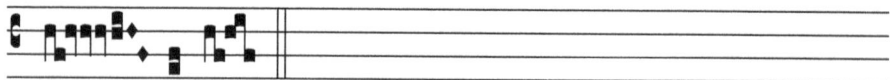

glad in it.

without the Neuma.

Then let the Priest say.

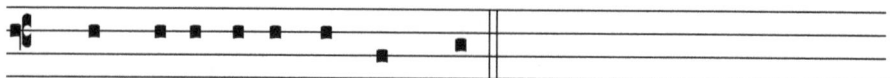

℣. In thy re-surrection, O Christ.

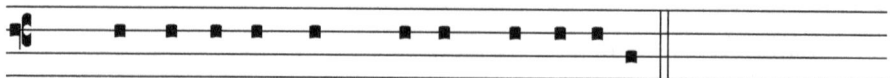

℟. Let heaven and earth re-joice, al-le-lu-ya.

℣. The Lord be with you. ℟. And with thy spirit. 62.

℣. Let us pray.

Prayer. Pour forth upon us. 35. *with* The Lord be with you. *and* Let us bless the Lord. 63. *without* Alleluya.

Compline is said in the same way through the whole week until Saturday.

Compline 14.

⁋ *On Sunday in the Octave of Easter at Compline* Turn us, O God. *and* O God, make speed to save me. Gloria Patri. *&c.* 1.

Alleluya. iiij.

Ant.
VIII.i.

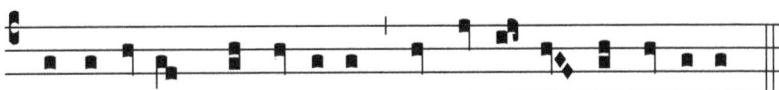

L-le-lu-ya, * al-le-lu-ya, al-le-lu- ya, al-le-lu-ya.

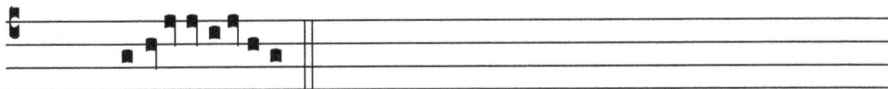

Ps. Hear me when I call. In thee, O Lord. Whoso dwelleth.

Behold now. 3.

Chapter. Thou. O Lord. 6.

Jesu salvator seculi.

Hymn.
VIII.

E- su, who brought'st re-demption nigh, * Word of

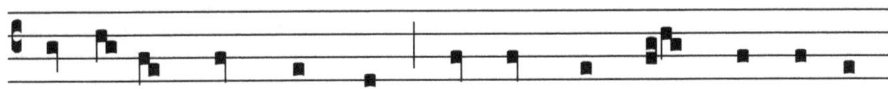

the Father, God most high : O Light of Light, to man un-

known, And watchful Guardian of thine own. 2. Thy hand

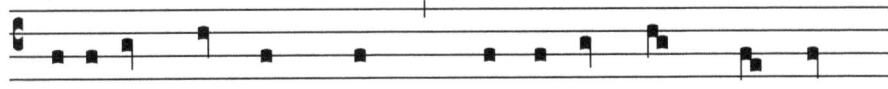

Cre-ation made and guides, Thy wisdom time from time

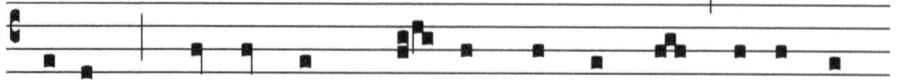

di-vides : By this world's cares and toils opprest, O give our

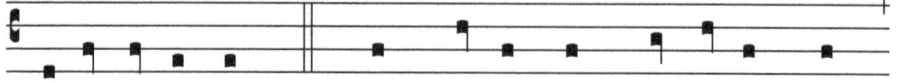

weary bodies rest. 3. That, while in frames of sin and pain

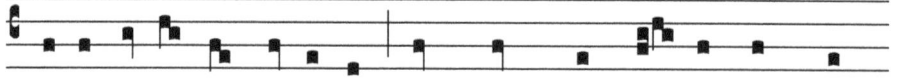

A little longer we remain, Our flesh may here in such wise

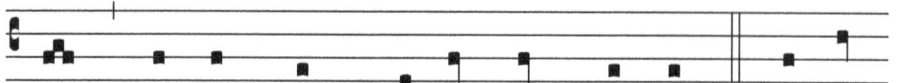

sleep, That watch with Christ our souls may keep. 4. O free

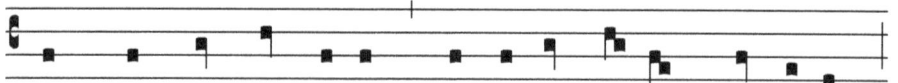

us, while we dwell be-low, From insults of our ghostly foe,

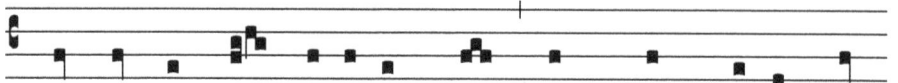

That he may ne'er victorious be   O'er them that are re-

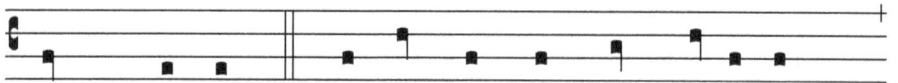

deemed by thee. 5. We pray thee, King with glo-ry decked,

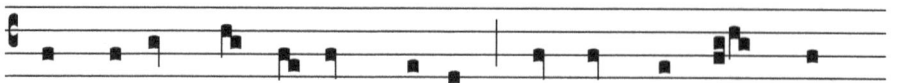

In this our Paschal joy, pro-tect From all that death would

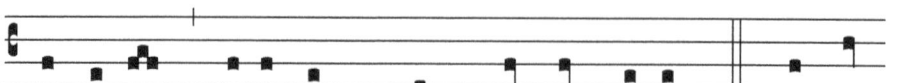

fain effect, Thy ransomed flock, thine own e-lect. 6. To thee

38

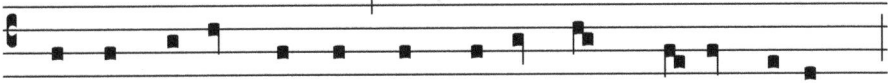

who, dead, a-gain dost live, All glo-ry, Lord, thy people give ;

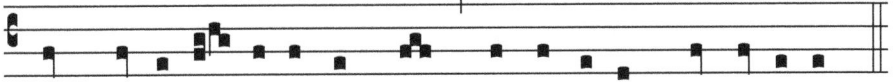

All glo-ry, as   is ev-er meet, To Father and to Pa-raclete.

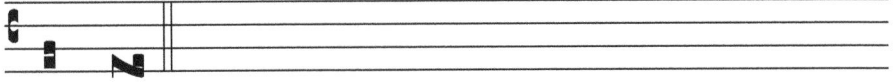

A- men.

℣. Keep us, O Lord. 9.

Alleluya.   Resurrexit Dominus.

Ant.
V.i.

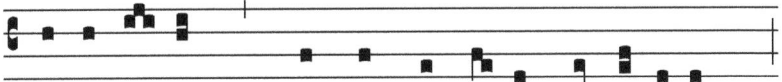

L-le-lu- ya. * The Lord is ri-sen, al-le-lu-ya :

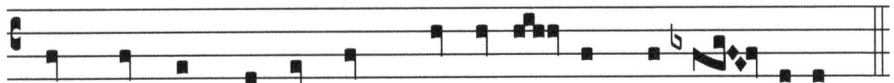

as   he   said   unto   you,   al-le-lu- ya,   al-le- lu-ya.

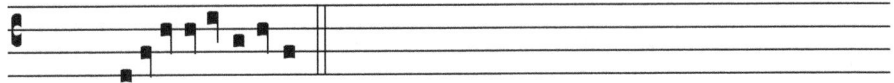

Ps. Lord, now lettest. 10.

Let the Preces &c. that pertain to Compline conclude the service. 55.

Let this Compline not be changed until the Ascension of the Lord, whatever the service be : except when it is said of Saint Mary : then indeed at the end of the Hymn is sung the Verse We pray thee, King. *with the* ℣.

6. All honour, laud, and glo-ry be, O Je-su, Vir-gin-born, to

thee ; All glo-ry, as is ev-er meet, To Father and to

Pa-raclete. A- men.

Such that the Antiphon on the Psalms is sung until the Feast of the Holy Trinity.

Compline 15.

❡ *On the Vigil of the Ascension of the Lord at Compline the Antiphon on the Psalms is as on the Octave of Easter.* 37.

Ps. When I called. *and the Psalms that follow.* 3.

Chapter. Thou, O Lord. 6.

Jesu nostra redemptio.

Hymn.
IV.

E-su, Re-demption all di-vine, * Whom here we love,

for whom we pine : God, working out Cre-ation's plan,

And in the lat-ter time, made man. 2. What love of thine

was that, which led To take our woes upon thy head,

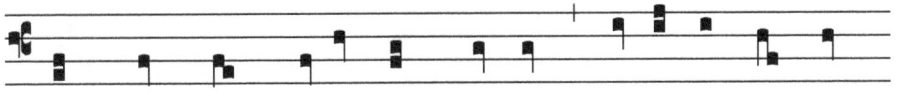

And pangs and cru-el death to bear, To ransom us from

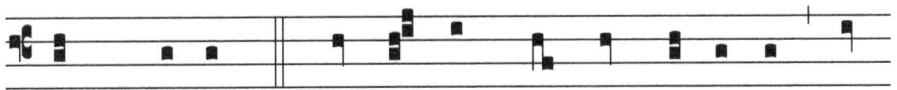

death's despair. 3. To thee hell's gate gave ready way, De-

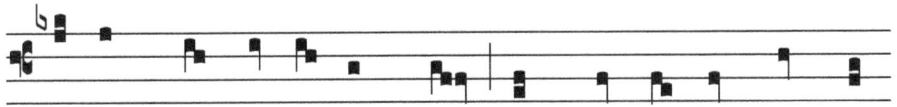

manding there his cap-tive prey : And now, in pomp and vic-

tor's pride, Thou sittest at the Father's side. 4. Let ve-ry

mer-cy force thee still To spare us, conquering all our ill ;

And, granting that we ask, on high With thine own face to

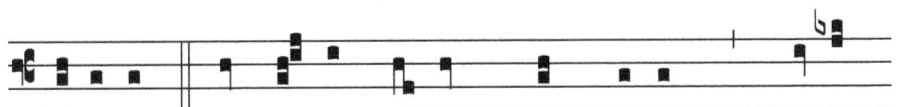

sa-tisfy. 5. Be thou our joy and strong de-fence, Who art

our fu-ture re-compense : So shall the light that springs

from thee Be ours through all e-terni-ty. 6. All glo-ry, Lord,

to thee we pay, Ascending o'er the stars to-day ; All glo-ry,

as is ev-er meet, To Father and to Pa-raclete. A- men.

℣. Keep us, O Lord. 9.

Alleluya. Ascendens Christus.

Ant.
V.i.

L-le-lu- ya. * Christ is gone up on high, al-le-

lu-ya : and hath led capti-vi-ty captive, al-le-lu- ya,

al-le- lu-ya. *Ps.* Lord, now lettest. 10.

Compline is sung in the same way daily until Pentecost whatever the service, except when a Commemoration of Blessed Mary is said : then indeed after the Verse Be thou our joy. *is sung the Verse.*

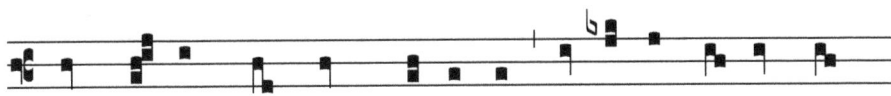

6. All ho-nour, laud, and glo-ry be, O Je-su, Vir-gin-born,

to thee ; All glo-ry, as is ev-er meet, To Father and to

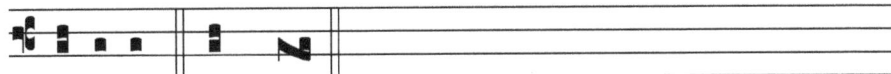

Pa-raclete. A- men.

Let the Preces &c. that pertain to Compline conclude the service. 55.

Compline 16.

❡ *On the Vigil of Pentecost at Compline the Antiphon* Alleluya. *iiij. as above in the Octave of Easter. 37.*

Ps. Hear me when I call. *and the Psalms that follow. 3.*

Chapter. Thou, O Lord. 6.

Hymn. Thee, Saviour of the world. 11.

℣. Keep us, O Lord. 9.

Alleluya. Spiritus Paraclitus.

Ant.
V.i.

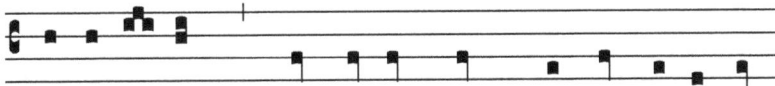

L-le-lu- ya. * The Ho-ly Ghost, the Comforter, al-

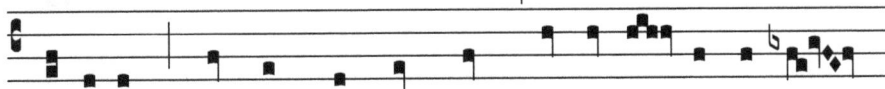

le-lu-ya : shall teach you all things, al-le-lu- ya, al-le-

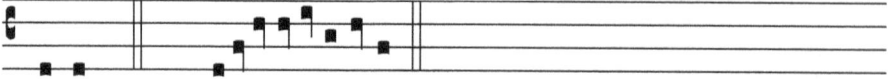

lu-ya. *Ps.* Lord, now lettest. 10.

Let the Preces &c. that pertain to Compline conclude the service. 55.

Compline 17.

❡ *On the Day of Pentecost at Compline the Antiphon* Alleluya. *iiij. as above.* 37.

Ps. Hear me when I call. *and the Psalms that follow.* 3.

Chapter. Thou, O Lord. 6.

On this day and the three days that follow in place of the Hymn is sung this Sequence.

Alma chorus Domini.

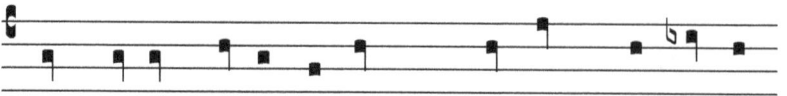

OW let our voices re-hearse * the Lord's dear ti-tles

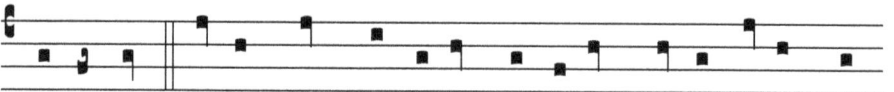

in order. Saviour, Emma-nu-el, Sa-ba-oth, Ado-na-y, Mes-

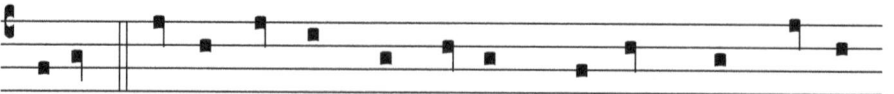

si-ah. Consubstantial, the Way and the Life, Hand, Only-

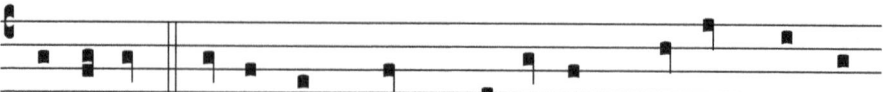

be-gotten. Wisdom and Might, Be-ginning, the First-born of

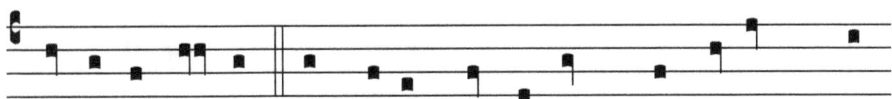

ev-e-ry crea-ture. Alpha and O we name Him, at once the

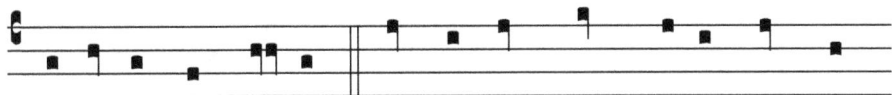

Be-ginning and Ending. Fountain and Source of all good, our

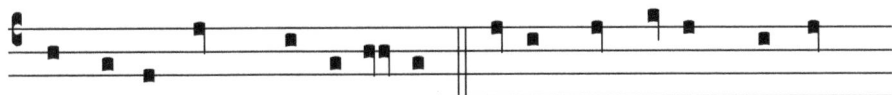

Advo-cate and Me-di- a- tor. He is the Heifer, the Lamb,

Sheep, Ram, the Worm, Serpent and Li- on. Mouth and

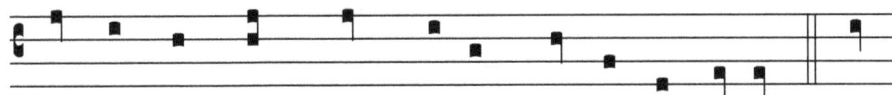

Word of God, Light, Sun, Glo-ry, Splendour and Image. Blos-

som, Bread, Vine, Door, Rock, Mountain and Stone of

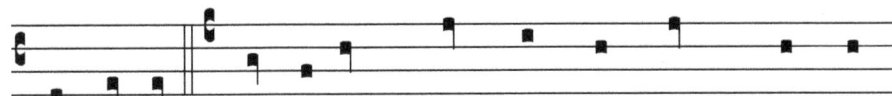

the Corner. Angel and Spouse of the Church, the Shep-

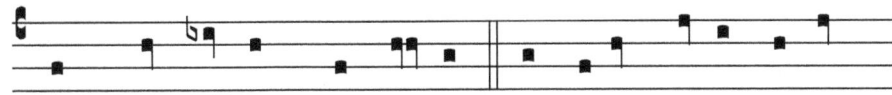

herd, the Priest and the Prophet. Mighty, Immortal, Supreme,

45

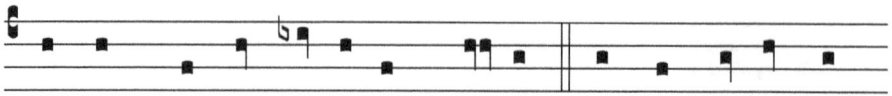

the Lord God Omni-po-tent, Je-sus. O may he save us,

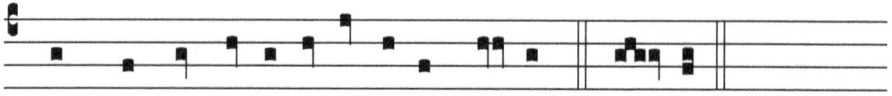

whose be the glo-ry for ev-er and ev-er, A-men.

On the remaining days however is sung the Hymn Thee, Saviour of the world. 11.

℣. Keep us, O Lord. 9.

Ant. Alleluya. The Holy Ghost. 44. *Ps.* Nunc dimittis. 10.

Let the Preces &c. that pertain to Compline conclude the service. 55.

Compline 18.

❡ *On the Feast of the Holy Trinity at Compline, Ant.* Have mercy. 3.

Ps. Hear me when I call. *and the Psalms that follow.* 3.

Chapter. Thou, O Lord. 6.

Hymn. Thee, Saviour of the World. 11.

℣. Keep us, O Lord. 9.

Lucem tuam.

Ant.
IV.ii.

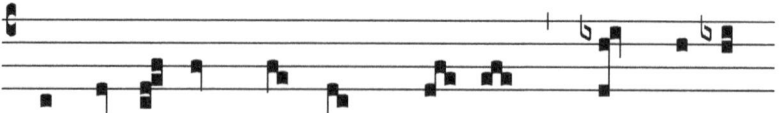

Rant unto us, * O Lord, thy light : that, the dark-

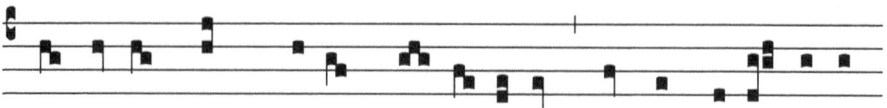

ness of our hearts be-ing pas-sed away, we may be a-ble to

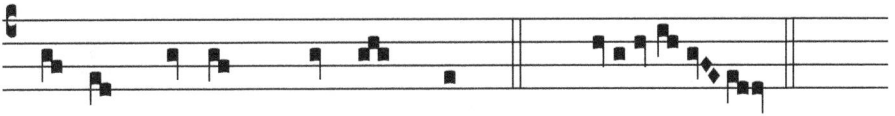

at-tain that light which is Christ. *Ps.* Lord, now lettest. 10.

Let the Preces &c. that pertain to Compline conclude the service. 55.

This Compline is said on all Double Feasts from this day until the Advent of the Lord : and from the Octave of the Epiphany until the first Sunday of Lent, except on the Feasts and during the Octaves of the Name of Jesus and of Blessed Mary : and on the Feasts of Relics and All Saints. It is also sung on the Feast and during the Octave of the Dedication of the Church whatever service takes place : if it occurs outside of Advent, Lent, and Eastertide : and if it occurs during the summer or elsewhere when the Octave can be celebrated with Rulers of the Choir then Compline is said as on the Feast itself.

Compline 19.

❡ *On the Feasts of Relics and All Saints at Compline on the Psalms.*
Sanctorum precibus.

Ant.
VIII.i.

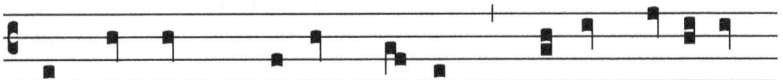

A T the prayers * of all the Saints, bestow salvation

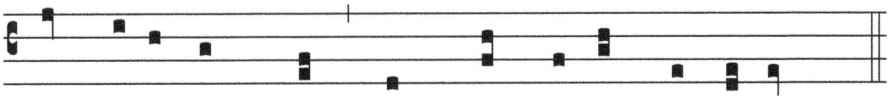

of body and mind, O Christ, unto thy servants.

Ps. Hear me when I call. *and the Psalms that follow. 3.*

Chapter. Thou, O Lord. 6.

Hymn. Thee, Saviour of the world. 11.

℣. Keep us, O Lord. 9.

Ant. Grant unto us, O Lord. 46.

Ps. Nunc dimittis. 10.

Let the Preces &c. that pertain to Compline conclude the service. 55.

Compline 20.

❡ *On the Purification of St. Mary at Compline on the Psalms.*

Virgo verbo.

Ant.
II.i.

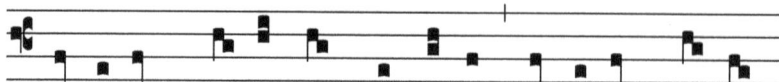

Virgin * by a word conceived, a Virgin she re-

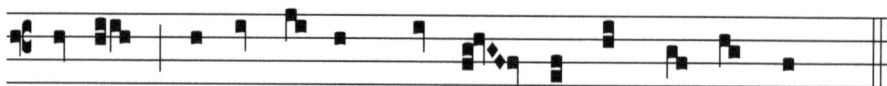

mained : as a Vir-gin she bare the King of all kings.

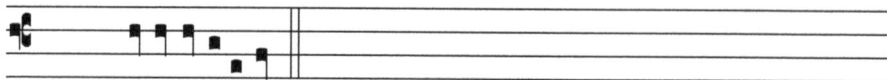

Ps. Hear me when I call. *and the Psalms that follow.* 3.

Chapter. Thou, O Lord. 6.

Hymn. Thee, Saviour of the world. 11.

℣. Keep us, O Lord. 9.

Ant. We glorify thee. 50.

Ps. Nunc dimittis. 10.

Let the Preces &c. that pertain to Compline conclude the service. 55.

Compline 21.

⊄ *On the Visitation and the Assumption of St. Mary at Compline on the Psalms.*

Sancta Maria.

Ant.
VIII.i.

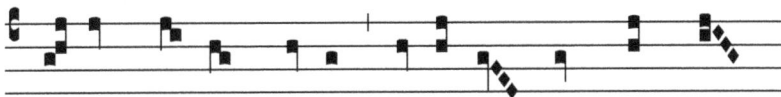

O-ly * Vir-gin Ma-ry,   intercede for the whole

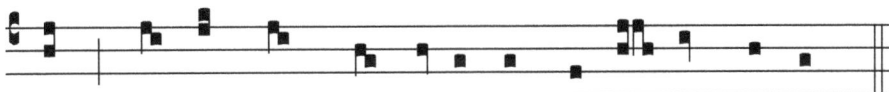

world : for he whom thou bar-est is the King of the world.

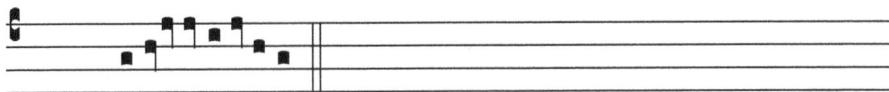

Ps. Hear me when I call. *and the Psalms that follow.* 3.

Chapter. Thou, O Lord. 6.

Hymn. Thee, Saviour of the world. 11.

℣. Keep us, O Lord. 9.

Ant. We glorify thee. 50.

Ps. Nunc dimittis. 10.

Let the Preces &c. that pertain to Compline conclude the service. 55.

Compline 22.

⊄ *On the Nativity of the same at Compline on the Psalms.*

Beata mater.

Ant.
II.i.

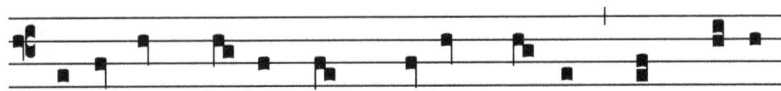

blessed Mother * and spotless Vir-gin, most glo-ri-

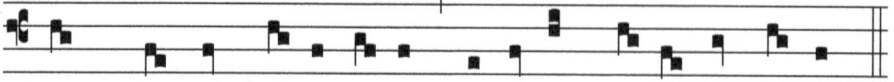

ous Queen of the u-ni-verse, intercede for us to the Lord.

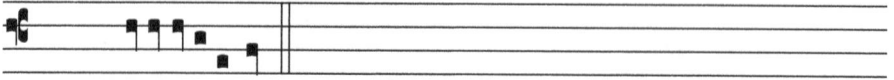

Ps. Hear me when I call. *and the Psalms that follow.* 3.

Chapter. Thou, O Lord. 6.
Hymn. Thee, Saviour of the world. 11.
℣. Keep us, O Lord. 9.

Glorificamus te.

Ant.
IV.iii.

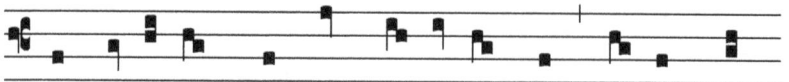

E glo-ri-fy * thee, O Mother of God, for of thee

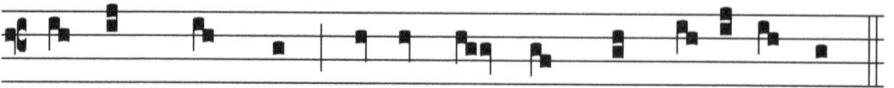

was born the Christ : succour all them that glo-ri-fy thee.

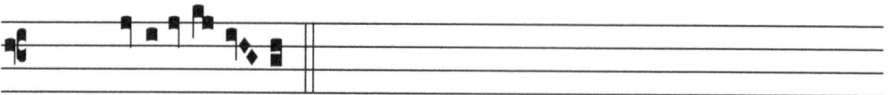

Ps. Lord, now lettest. 10.

Let the Preces &c. that pertain to Compline conclude the service. 55.

The preceding Antiphon, that is We glorify thee. *is sung on all Feasts and during Octaves of Blessed Mary, and on Commemorations of the same, through the whole year, except in Advent, and on the Annunciation of the Lord, and in Eastertide.*

Compline 23.

❡ *On the Feast of the Holy Name of Jesus at Compline on the Psalms.*
Miserere michi Domine secundum judicium.

Ant.
VIII.i.

HAve mercy * upon me, O Lord, as thou

us-est to do unto those that love thy Name.

Ps. Hear me when I call. *and the Psalms that follow.* 3.

Chapter. Thou, O Lord. 6.

Alma chorus Domini.

Seq.
VIII.

NOW let our voices re-hearse * the Lord's dear ti-tles

in order. Saviour, Emma-nu-el, Sa-ba-oth, Ado-na-y, Mes-

si-ah. Consubstantial, the Way and the Life, Hand, Only-be-gotten. Wisdom and Might, Be-ginning, the First-born of

ev-e-ry crea-ture. Alpha and O we name Him, at once the

Be-ginning and Ending. Fountain and Source of all good, our

Advo-cate and Me-di- a- tor. He is the Heifer, the Lamb,

Sheep, Ram, the Worm, Serpent and Li- on. Mouth and

Word of God, Light, Sun, Glo-ry, Splendour and Image. Blos-

som, Bread, Vine, Door, Rock, Mountain and Stone of

the Corner.   Angel and Spouse of the Church, the Shep-

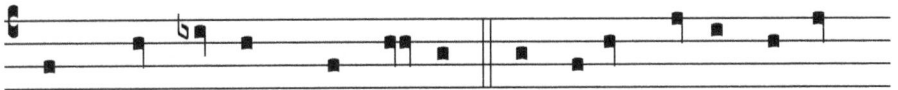

herd, the Priest and the Prophet. Mighty, Immortal, Supreme,

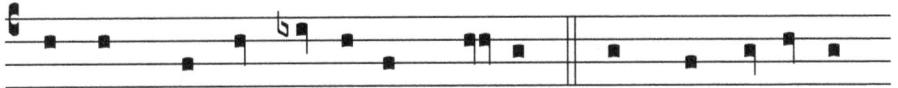

the Lord God Omni-po-tent, Je-sus. These be thy ti-tles,

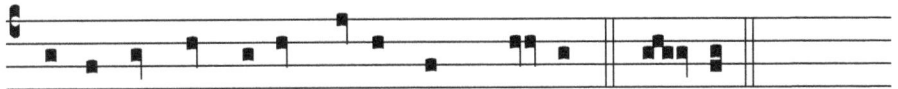

Je-su, to thee be all honour and glo-ry.   A-men.

℣. Keep us, O Lord. 9.

O Rex gloriose.

Ant.
III.iv.

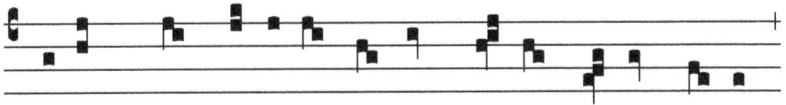

King, * all glo-ri-ous a-mid thy saintly compa-ny,

who ev-er shalt be praised, yet exceedest all ut-ter-ance :

thou, O Lord, art in the midst of us, and we are cal-led

by thy ho-ly Name ; leave us not, O our God : that in the

day of judgement it may please thee to place us a-

mong thy saints and cho-sen ones, O blessed King.

Ps. Lord, now lettest. 10.

Let the Preces &c. that pertain to Compline conclude the service. 55.

This Compline is not altered during the whole of the Octave when the service is of the Octave.

❡ *Here follow the Preces.*

When the Antiphon is finished the Preces follow, beginning with the Choir Side, and let them be begun by a lesser person thus, and they are sung in alternation.

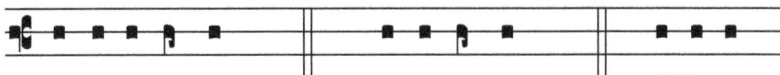

K Y-ri- e-léyson. *iij.* Christe-léyson. *iij.* Ky-ri- e-

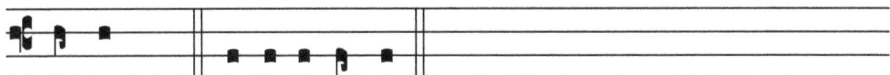

léyson. *ij.* Ky-ri- e-léyson.

or

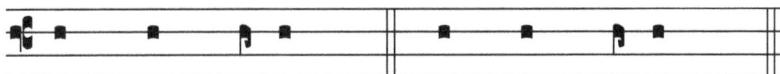

L Ord, have mercy. *iij.* Christ, have mercy. *iij.*

Lord, have mercy. *ij.* Lord, have mercy.

And let the Choir then say secretly :

OUr Father, which art in heaven, hallowed be thy Name. Thy kingdom come. Thy will be done in earth as it is in heaven. Give us this day our daily bread. And forgive us our trespasses, as we forgive them that trespass against us. And lead us not into temptation, but deliver us from evil. Amen.

HAil Mary, full of grace, the Lord is with thee. Blessed art thou among women, and blessed is the fruit of thy womb, Jesus Christ. (Holy Mary, Mother of God, pray for us sinners, now and at the hour of death.) | Amen.

Then let the Priest say.

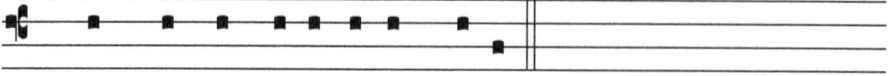

℣. And lead us not into temptation.

Let the Choir respond.

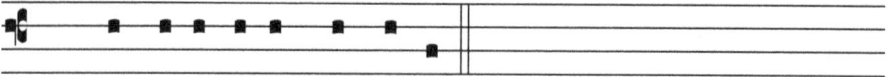

℟. But de-li-ver us from e-vil.

The Priest.

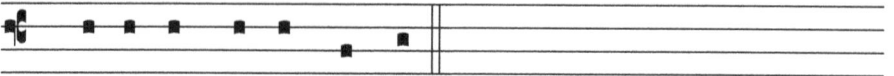

℣. I will lay me down in peace.

Let the Choir respond.

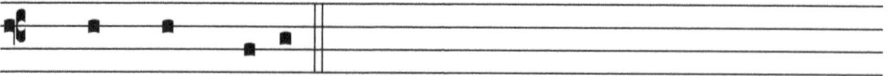

℟. And take my rest.

Secretly :

I believe in God the Father Almighty, Maker of heaven and earth. And in Jesus Christ his only Son our Lord. Who was conceived by the Holy Ghost, born of the Virgin Mary, suffered under Pontius Pilate, was crucified, dead, and buried. He descended into hell. The third day he rose again from the dead. He ascended into heaven, and sitteth on the right hand of God the Father Almighty. From thence he shall come to judge the quick and the dead.

I believe in the Holy Ghost, the holy catholick Church, the communion of saints, the forgiveness of sins, the resurrection of the body, and the life everlasting. Amen.

Then let the Verses be sung and responded to likewise under the same Tone.

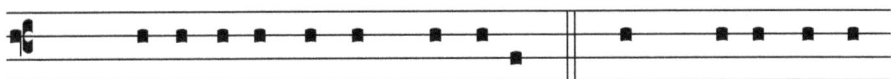

℣. The re-surrection of the body.   ℟. And the life ev-er-

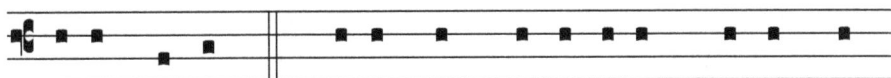

lasting. Amen.   ℣. Let us bless the Father and the Son, with

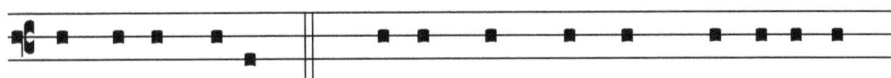

the Ho-ly Spi-rit.   ℟. Let us praise him, and magni-fy him

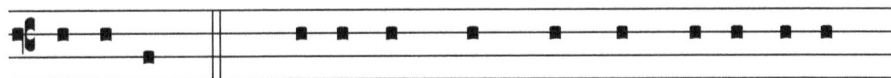

for ev-er.   ℣. Blessed art thou, Lord, in the firmament

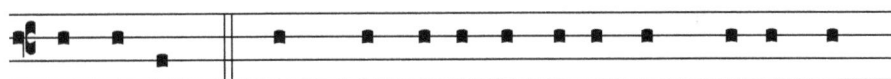

of heaven.   ℟. And worthy to be praised, and glorious, and

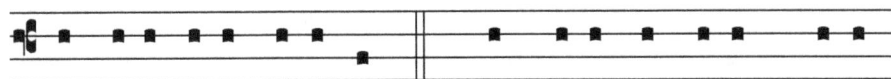

highly ex-alted for ev-er.   ℣. May the Almighty and merci-

ful Lord bless and pre-serve us.   ℟. Amen.

❡ *It noted that the Priest of greatest dignity then says* Confiteor. &c. *whether at Prime or at Compline throughout the whole year when the* Confiteor. *is said. And it is said privately, that is so that it can barely be heard by the Choir, firstly this way, facing the Altar.*

Confiteor.

I confess to God, to blessed Mary, to all the saints, *Turning to the Choir* and to you, that I have sinned exceedingly : in thought, word, and deed, through my own fault. *Turning to the Altar while is said* I beseech holy Mary, all the saints of God, *Turning to the Choir while is said* and you to pray for me.

Let the Choir respond, facing him.

Misereatur.

May almighty God have mercy upon thee and forgive thee all thy sins : deliver thee from every evil : preserve and strengthen thee in goodness and bring thee to everlasting life. *Let the Priest respond,* Amen.

The Choir facing the Altar.

Confiteor.

I confess to God, to blessed Mary, to all the saints, *Turning to the Choir* and to you, that I have sinned exceedingly : in thought, word, and deed, through my own fault. *Turning to the Altar while is said* I beseech holy Mary, all the saints of God, *Turning to the Priest while is said* and thee to pray for me.

Then, facing the Choir, let the Priest say.

Misereatur.

May almighty God have mercy upon you and forgive you all your sins, deliver you from every evil, preserve and strengthen you in goodness and bring you to everlasting life. *Let the Choir respond,* Amen.

The Priest.

Absolutionem.

THE almighty and merciful Lord grant you absolution and remission of all your sins, time for true repentance, amendment of life, and the grace and consolation of the Holy Ghost. *Let the Choir respond,* Amen.

❡ *In the absence of a Priest : the Choir, facing the Altar.*

I confess to God, to blessed Mary, to all the saints, *Turning to the Choir* and to you, that I have sinned exceedingly : in thought, word, and deed, through my own fault. *Turning to the Altar while is said* I beseech Holy Mary, all the saints of God, and you *Turning to the Choir while is said* to pray for me.

MAy almighty God have mercy upon us and forgive us all our sins, deliver us from every evil, preserve and strengthen us in goodness and bring us to everlasting life. Amen.

❡ *If it is said by only one.*

I confess to God, to blessed Mary, and to all the saints, that I have sinned exceedingly : in thought, word, and deed, through my own fault. I beseech Holy Mary and all the saints of God to pray for me.

MAy almighty God have mercy upon me and forgive me all my sins, deliver me from every evil, preserve and strengthen me in goodness and bring me to everlasting life. Amen.

❡ *Throughout the whole year when* Confiteor. *is said let the following Preces be sung by the officiating Priest this way.*

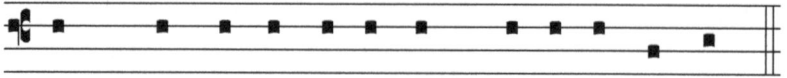

WILT thou not turn a-gain and quicken us, O God ?

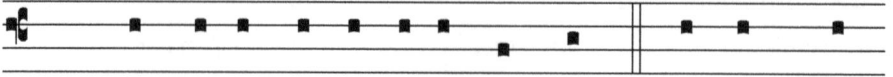

℟. That thy people may re-joice in thee. ℣. O Lord, shew

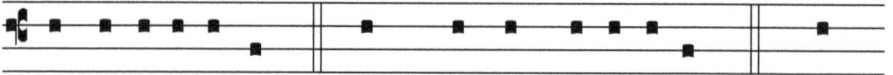

thy mercy upon us. ℟. And grant us thy salvation. ℣. Vouch-

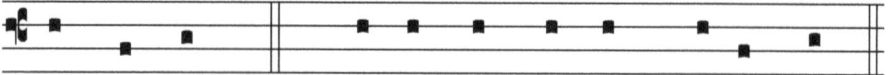

safe, O Lord. ℟. To keep us this night without sin.

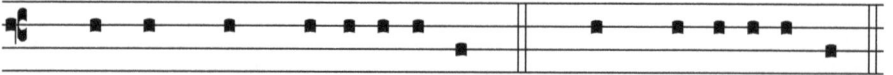

℣. O Lord, have mercy upon us. ℟. Have mercy upon us.

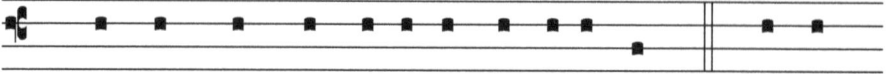

℣. O Lord, let thy mercy lighten upon us. ℟. As our

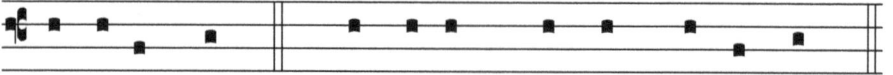

trust is in thee. ℣. Turn us again, O Lord God of hosts.

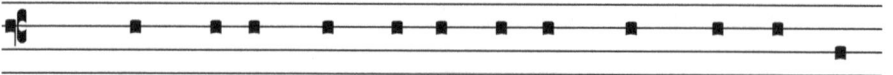

℟. Shew the light of thy counte-nance, and we shall be

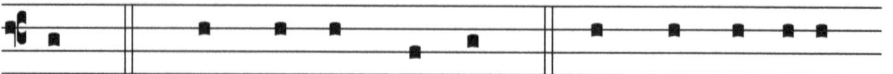

whole. ℣. Hear my prayer, O Lord. ℟. And let my cry- ing

come unto thee. ℣. The Lord be with you. ℟. And with

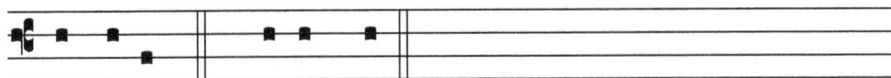

thy spi-rit. ℣. Let us pray.

The preceding Preces are sung in the above manner throughout the whole year at Compline whether on Double Feasts or on Simples and also without Rulers of the Choir, and on ferias except from Maundy Thursday until the Octave of Easter : in such a way that on all ferias in Advent, and from Domine ne in ira. *until Maundy Thursday, and from the* Deus omnium. *until the Advent of the Lord, when service is of the feria, after the* ℣. O Lord, let thy mercy. &c. (*) *there follows immediately this Versicle thus.*

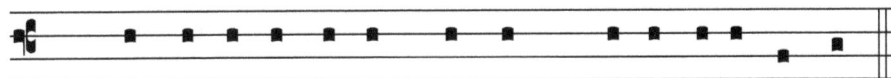

℣. Hearken unto my voice, O Lord, when I cry unto thee.

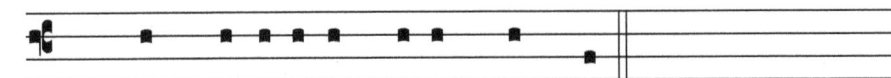

℟. Have mercy upon me, and hear me.

And immediately let be begun by the Choir Side this Psalm Have mercy upon me. *The whole Psalm is said with* Gloria Patri. *without note, alternating Verses in the Choir.*

Psalm 51. Miserere mei Deus. l.

Ave mercy upon me, O God, after thy great goodness : according to the multitude of thy mercies do away mine offences.

2. Wash me throughly from my wickedness : and cleanse me from my sin.

3. For I acknowledge my faults : and my sin is ever before me.

4. Against thee only have I sin-

ned, and done this evil in thy sight : that thou mightest be justified in thy saying, and clear when thou art judged.

5. Behold, I was shapen in wickedness : and in sin hath my mother conceived me.

6. But lo, thou requirest truth in the inward parts : and shalt make me to understand wisdom secretly.

7. Thou shalt purge me with hyssop, and I shall be clean : thou shalt wash me, and I shall be whiter than snow.

8. Thou shalt make me hear of joy and gladness : that the bones which thou hast broken may rejoice.

9. Turn thy face from my sins : and put out all my misdeeds.

10. Make me a clean heart, O God : and renew a right spirit within me.

11. Cast me not away from thy presence : and take not thy holy Spirit from me.

12. O give me the comfort of thy help again : and stablish me with thy free Spirit.

13. Then shall I teach thy ways unto the wicked : and sinners shall be converted unto thee.

14. Deliver me from blood-guiltiness, O God, thou that art the God of my health : and my tongue shall sing of thy right-eousness.

15. Thou shalt open my lips, O Lord : and my mouth shall shew thy praise.

16. For thou desirest no sacrifice, else would I give it thee : but thou delightest not in burnt-offerings.

17. The sacrifice of God is a troubled spirit : a broken and contrite heart, O God, shalt thou not despise.

18. O be favourable and gracious unto Sion : build thou the walls of Jerusalem.

19. Then shalt thou be pleased with the sacrifice of righteousness, with the burnt-offerings and ob-lations : then shall they offer young bullocks upon thine altar.

Glory be to the Father, and to

the Son : and to the Holy Ghost. As it was in the beginning, is | now, and ever shall be : world without end. Amen.

And then let all be said kneeling from the beginning of the first Kyrie eleyson. *until after the Prayer and* Confiteor. *and* Misereatur. *and* Absolutionem. *in such a way that immediately after the Psalm* Miserere. *let the Priest alone arise singing thus.*

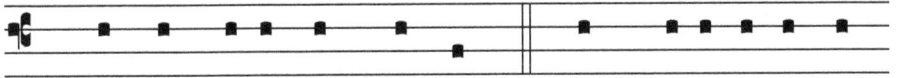

℣. O Lord, a-rise and help us. ℟. And de-li-ver us for

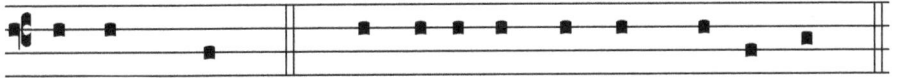

thy Name's sake. ℣. Turn us a-gain, O Lord God of hosts.

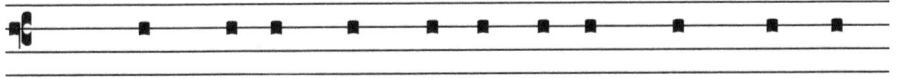

℟. Shew the light of thy counten-ance, and we shall

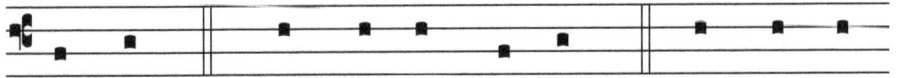

be whole. ℣. Hear my prayer, O Lord. ℟. And let my

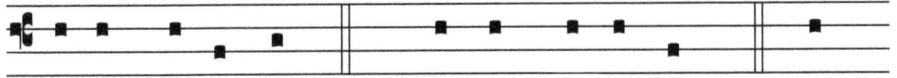

cry come unto thee. ℣. The Lord be with you. ℟. And

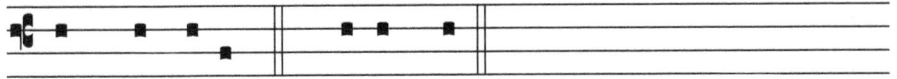

with thy spi-rit. ℣. Let us pray.

Prayer.

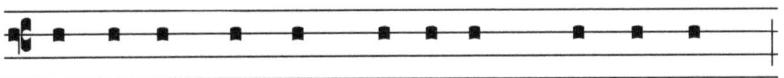

Ighten our darkness, we be-seech thee, O Lord :

63

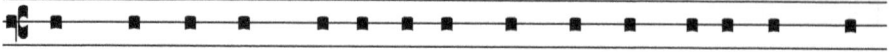

and by thy great mercy de-fend us from all pe-rils and dan-

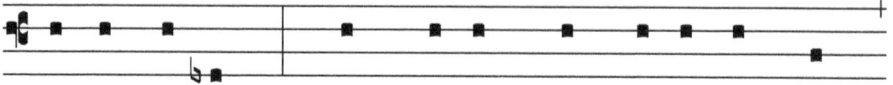

gers of this night. Through Je-sus Christ thy Son, our Lord,

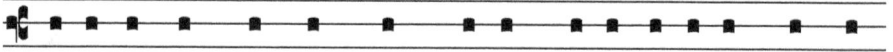

who liv-eth and reigneth with thee in the u-ni-ty of the Ho-

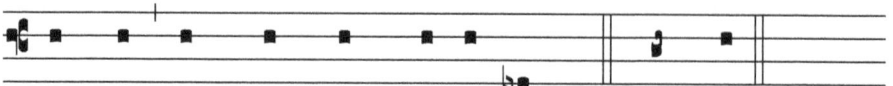

ly Ghost, one God, world without end. ℟. A- men.

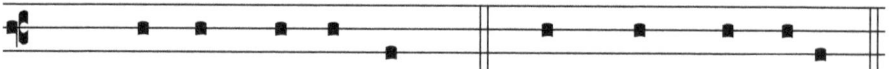

℣. The Lord be with you. ℟. And with thy spi-rit.

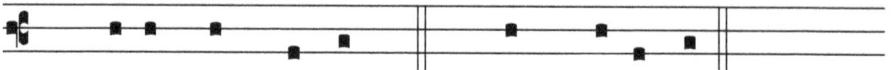

℣. Let us bless the Lord. ℟. Thanks be to God.

Let the preceding Prayer together with the aforesaid Chapter and the ℣. Keep us, O Lord. be said at Compline throughout the whole year, except from Maundy Thursday until the Octave of Easter, and except on All Souls' Day.

For the Peace of the Church.

⁋ *It is noted that every day of the year after Compline of the day : except on Double Feasts and except during the Octaves of Corpus Christi and the Visitation, the Assumption and the Nativity of Blessed Mary, and the Dedication of the Church, and the Name of Jesus, and on All Souls' Day, and on the Vigil of the Nativity of the Lord, and from then until the beginning of the history* Domine ne in ira. *and from the Wednesday before Easter until the beginning of the history* Deus omnium. *the following Psalm is said for the Peace of the Church while kneeling and without note.*

Psalm 123. Ad te levavi oculos meos. cxxij.

𝖀Nto thee lift I up mine eyes : O thou that dwellest in the heavens.

2. Behold, even as the eyes of servants : look unto the hand of their masters.

3. And as the eyes of a maiden unto the hand of her mistress : even so our eyes wait upon the Lord our God, until he have mercy upon us.

4. Have mercy upon us, O Lord, have mercy upon us : for we are utterly despised.

5. Our soul is filled with the scornful reproof of the wealthy : and with the despitefulness of the proud.

Glory be to the Father, and to the Son : and to the Holy Ghost.

As it was in the beginning, is now, and ever shall be : world without end. Amen.

⁋ *The Psalm being finished, let follow.*

℣. Kyrie eleyson.

℟. Christe eleyson.

℣. Kyrie eleyson.

or

℣. Lord, have mercy.

℟. Christ, have mercy.

℣. Lord, have mercy.

℣. Our Father. Hail Mary. 55. *privately.*

⁋ *Then let the officiating Priest say audibly but without note, while kneeling.*

℣. And lead us not into temptation.

℟. But deliver us from evil.

℣. O Lord, arise and help us.

℟. And deliver us for thy Name's sake.

℣. Turn us again, O Lord God of hosts.

℟. Shew the light of thy countenance, and we shall be whole.

℣. O Lord hear my prayer.

℟. And let my cry come unto thee.

℣. The Lord be with you.

℟. And with thy spirit.

℣. Let us pray.

Then let the officiating Priest say aloud but without note, likewise kneeling.

Prayer.

Favourably receive, (we beseech thee,) O Lord, the prayers of thy Church : that being delivered from all adversities and errors, she may safely serve thee in freedom, and grant us thy peace in all our days. Through Christ our Lord. ℟. Amen.

❧ *This said, let the Priest and all the Clerks arise from prostration, kissing the Forms.*

www.ingramcontent.com/pod-product-compliance
Lightning Source LLC
Chambersburg PA
CBHW030758150426
42813CB00068B/3210/J